AS IT WAS IN THE BEGINNING

by marie glen

ISBN: 978-0-615-23587-5

CONTENTS: Page:

CHAPTER 1 ~ THE FOUR GOSPELS

As we spin and revolve at breakneck speed through the universe, there comes a time to each one of us, when we want to stand still upon this spinning orb and seek the answers to the big questions of life – who are we? What is life? In our quest, surely we might want to acquaint our self just a little with the ancient story of the soft spoken man from Nazareth. What were his words, message and advice? And what is the promise the bible claims? We can merely accept the present day popular claim that the historical records are unreliable, and dismiss them as mere myth, and remain unaware of the highly interesting and inspiring writings of some everyday people written long ago over a span of centuries of life...

1

There's much mystery in the world, and the mystery, so long ago named "the good news" came to stand in the world every bit as monumental as the pyramids of Egypt, and the giant statues of Easter Island do. Its setting was the world of everyday working men and women. There are four testimonies, or accounts, which were penned by unknown average people of the day. The story they communicated turned much of the world upside down. It is full of drama and it makes large claims about life.

See a small fishing boat, peacefully floating and anchored in the harbor of a small town. Nearby we see where it all begins, with a quiet and gentle, yet regular looking fellow, walking down dusty streets. He is followed by crowds of people, of all ages, who jostle each other and excitedly strain to hear his every word. For he tells them wonderful things which lift them entirely out of their harsh exacting world. A world which has been made more gray by the boots of a foreign army stirring up the dust of their hometown streets.

Not only does he speak wondrous things, and make wonderful promises and claims, but he lives right among the people and is one of them. His glance is full of familiarity, good will and affection. His teachings seem like manna from heaven, his lessons like ambrosia. His presence is said to chase away dire sicknesses, and handicaps, and to restore the minds of those lost in madness! But still, he lives a humble life among the town and the families. Children love to sit by him and follow him around. He and his brothers had inherited their father's carpentry skill and trade. But soon enough he began to teach.

He was known to speak quietly and

softly, with the words he spoke being built upon well known historical events, which were sometimes accompanied by great booms of thunder and crackling lightning strikes, even earthquake.. Words etched in stone by the very finger of God.. Of Moses coming down off the mountain with the stone tablets, his hair bleached white as snow. Of Jacob resting his head in sleep upon a rock, and dreaming of a mighty staircase, connecting heaven and earth, and radiant angels going to and fro upon "Jacob's ladder".. And of God saying to Jacob, I will reveal my plan.. my promise to man, and I will seal it, and guarantee it with a pledge.. And stamp it too with thunderings, lightning, earthquake, and things never before seen. A promise as solid as rock, was the claim.

As the man of Bethlehem and Nazareth walked along, he found twelve men he invited to walk with him. They dropped what they were doing and followed him. Most of them were fishermen, but there was even a tax collector in their group, named Matthew, who though he belonged to one of the twelve tribes of Israel, he collected taxes for the hated enemy. Rome! But Matthew left his tax collecting, and they all became a traveling band of brothers, for being around Jesus was changing each one of them, and changing their attitudes and divisions.

Sometimes they had "no where to lay their heads" at night. Other times they stayed in Peter's house, where his wife and mother also lived. Sometimes they slept under the stars and moon, especially when they were near Jerusalem, and would sleep in the park at the nearby Mount of Olives. When they visited the towns, everyone came out to

5

listen to Jesus, and they brought their sick folk out to him, and he would touch them. On Sabbath day he would go to the small town synagogue and listen to the reading of the parchment of God, or read from it. But he was not as popular inside the synagogue as he was outside in the streets and byways of the town.

After awhile, it got to be such a stir when he came around that he had to stop coming into the towns, but stayed outside the towns and the townspeople would look for him. Sometimes they would follow him to another town, or down by the large lake, called Galilee, around which many of the towns were located. Some of the men's fishing boats came in handy, for they not only used them from time to time to reach another town, but Jesus liked to pull a boat near to shore and teach from it. Many days he spoke as they sat at the side of a hill, or walked along the seashore.

One or two times they even went fishing. The men used large nets to fish with, and it had always been a profitable enough trade. One day they fished as they always had, but all day long whenever they pulled in their net, it was empty. Peter was exasperated, and when Jesus said put the net down on the other side of the boat, he said "..but Lord, we've been fishing all day and have caught nothing!"

Jesus said "fish from the right side of the boat" and when they did and pulled in the net, they filled the boat with the fish, and the net nearly broke there was so many fish. Jesus told his friends their occupation would change, they would become fishers of men.

One day there was a large crowd of people who had been following him around for a couple of days, and he,

7

along with the disciples, wanted to give them something to eat, knowing that they would soon be feeling faint with hunger. Jesus had them all sit down in an orderly fashion and he gave thanks and broke apart a few loaves, a small fishing boy had given him, and had the disciples hand out the bread to the people, along with a few fish the little boy had also given. Everyone in the crowd ate til they were full! And quite a few baskets of left overs were picked up afterwards! That day was recorded as one of many happy and exciting days.

Another time, it got very late, and Jesus, who enjoyed time apart to pray and reflect in solitude, sent the disciples out across the lake in the boat, to the next town, while he walked alone for a bit. Soon it got late and the disciples rowing in the boat saw what they thought was a spirit walking out upon the water towards them. They were more than just a little afraid, until Jesus said "Don't be afraid. It's only me."

Peter, kind of an excitable guy, jumped up and said "Lord! Tell me to, and I'll come walking out upon the water too. Say so! And I'll be able to walk on the water."

So Jesus reached out his hand toward him and said "Come on then."

And Peter stepped out onto the water, and actually took a couple of steps. But the water was a bit choppy. They had even been struggling a bit in their rowing, which was probably why Jesus came to them in the first place. When Peter noticed, and was reminded of the waves, he suddenly became afraid and began to sink.

He cried out "Help Lord! I'm sinking!" But Jesus reached out his hand and pulled him up, and they both got into the boat.

And then they, and the boat were immediately at the shore, right where they had been headed.

When they went to Jerusalem, which was usually during the week of the three spring holy days, or for one of the fall holy days, Jesus would go to the temple and speak and teach, and do some healing there. One time, on his way to the city and through the gates, Jesus was riding on a young donkey and everyone began to lay palm branches in his path (like a red carpet) and they were singing "hosanna to the highest" and praising Jesus as God's only begotten (straight out from God) son and waving some of the palm branches as they sang.

Some said "tell these people and children to be quiet!"

But Jesus said, "If they weren't singing right now, the rocks would be.."

Soon enough, going to the cities got

to be dangerous. There were deep currents of antagonism and threats. To some, Jesus was just too popular with the people. They misunderstood his mission and motives. They thought of him as a wizard who was threatening their seats and status in life. Soon, one of Jesus' own disciples made a deal with them, and for thirty pieces of silver, agreed to tell them of a time and place where they could lay hands on him when he was away from the crowds.

Jesus knew all this, and he began to warn his disciples that he was going away. He even came right out and told them they were going to kill him. One day Peter said "Who's going to kill you Lord?" Not really believing him.

On the evening of Jesus' arrest, they had a meal in an upper room, which Jesus had arranged beforehand. It was the Passover supper, sometimes called

Sabbath, as holidays were sometimes called Sabbath. Israel's days always began at sunset. So as the sun was setting on this day, Passover day was beginning.

Jesus told them, "I have wanted to have this Passover meal with you." As they sat, or "reclined" at the table, which was the custom of the day, John, a close disciple and friend of Jesus who later called Jesus "the Word of God", leaned upon Jesus a few moments as they sat, for Jesus was as a beloved elder brother. It was at this time that Jesus confided to John "..he who dips his bread in the broth the same time I do, is the one who will betray me."

Jesus dipped his bread, and Judas, reached forward and dipped his bread in the bowl at the very same moment.

"Go and do what you must," Jesus told him. And Judas got up and left. The other disciples thought he had some financial matter to attend to, for he was the one who kept the purse.

At this supper, Jesus told them that he was the bread and wine of the sacred Passover supper, the Passover lamb, and also the sustenance, the daily spiritual bread and wine, of all who follow him, and trust his message, through all days, and on into the ages of eternity. And his Spirit, which would be "poured out" is the "new wine" far better and greater than any other wine there is in life. Later it was written, "just as in Adam all die, in Jesus, all will live".

The soldiers came later that same Passover night, and arrested Jesus, under the watching moon, in the garden of Gethsemane, the park at the mount of Olives.

"I spent the days with you openly" Jesus said, "and do you come out now as thieves to catch me?"

Peter grabbed a sword and cut off one of the soldiers ears, but Jesus touched the soldier's ear and healed it. And he went with them without any sort of struggle.

"My kingdom is not of this world" he said, "else mine own would come out with knives and swords to battle.."

"You don't understand what manner of kingdom it is" he said.

As we know, Jesus was put to death as a dangerous yet common criminal, upon a sturdy Roman cross, the empire's all too well known instrument of execution and intimidation.

It was the morning after his arrest, and still Passover when Jesus was judged and condemned, mostly by the leaders of his own people, though of course, any people, sadly, would have done the same thing. That is to say, history is all the

14

same story. But what a great thing to be recorded as the tiny humble nation that gave birth to "the savior of the world!"

Jesus hung on the cross the rest of that Passover day. He was between two other men, who were being executed also, although they were only thieves. One spat out insults, and was taunting Jesus, but the other one said "Have you no respect? We at least, are being crucified for breaking the law, but this man is innocent," and he said to Jesus, "remember me when you are in your Kingdom".

"I tell you today," Jesus said to him, "you will be with me in paradise.."

Later as the day waned on, and the religious leaders were becoming anxious for the next holiday or Sabbath meal, which would begin at sunset, the skies turned black, there was an earthquake and lightning, and Jesus died saying

"Father forgive them, they know not what they are doing," and "into your hands I commend my spirit."

As the sun was going down, and Passover holiday was ending, and the day of Unleavened Bread (sometimes just called Passover too) was beginning, some friends came inquiring after his body, and they put him in a tomb (cave) which belonged to one of the friends, and closed it up.

But three nights and three days later, the sun was going down, the regular weekly Sabbath had ended, and the third holy day of Holy Week had begun. A strong angel came, and rolled away the boulder from in front of the tomb, and Jesus arose, as he had told them he would, for he had been warning them for a few weeks that these things were going to happen.

It's recorded, the first person he

16

revealed himself to, early the next morning, was Mary Magdalene, a female disciple. When she told her brothers of his rising, they didn't believe her. A little later, as ten of them were gathered together on this Sabbath of Firstfruits, Jesus was suddenly in the room with them, but left before Thomas the eleventh came in.

When Thomas heard what had happened, he proclaimed, "Unless I can see his wounds with my own eyes, and touch them with my own hands, I don't believe such a thing!"

But Jesus came back, and said to Thomas "See my wounds, and reach out your hand, and touch them". The previously doubting Thomas had no trouble believing after that, and overcome with awe and joy, he fell to his knees, and said "my Lord!"

We know all these things, and some of

the words and lessons Jesus spoke, because some of these same disciples wrote these things down, or dictated them, or in one case, was interviewed about them. The four gospels of the New Testament are their testaments and testimonies. They were each written about twenty to forty years later. Minor mundane details, as in all eyewitness accounts, differ in their telling, but the very same story and message seems to shine through, claiming the grave was opened, and death was visibly triumphed over! They had seen him die, but after three nights and days in the "lower part of the earth" (the dust and the grave) they felt him, "and handled him with their own hands" and found he was "flesh and bone".

CHAPTER 2 ~ A BOOK OF "ACTS"

And so it was, that exactly seven weeks, or forty-nine days later, was another holiday, the late Spring feast, which stands alone, called "Pentecost". After his resurrection, the Lord had remained with them, teaching, for another forty days. Then they watched as he ascended upon a white cloud out of their sight and up into heaven, until two angels appeared and said "why do you stare up into heaven? This same one you saw go into heaven, shall be seen returning in the very same manner". And they went back to the city of Jerusalem, to await his promise, he had told them specifically to remain in Jerusalem and wait for.

It came nine days later. Once again

like thunder, lightning and earthquake, with a "mighty rushing wind" the promise came and filled the house where they were, with individual flames of fire (and inspiration) over each one! It was the Holy Ghost! The very Spirit of God, supernatural, come to abide with them, guide them, inspire and empower them, the same Spirit Jesus had, and had promised would be "poured out". They went outside into the public square, and though unlearned men, spoke the languages of all the foreigners around them! So that every person heard the message in their own language. And Peter stood in the square outside the temple, and explained all these mysteries to the crowd which had gathered in Jerusalem, not only for the previous day of the weekly Sabbath, but for the great crowd there for the holiday of Pentecost.

Three thousand persons joined the

group's number that day. And from that day, the weak, even fearful group of students (or disciples) who had scattered into hiding the night of Jesus' arrest, became teachers (or apostles) and became energetically and courageously emboldened, and went out and changed all the world around them, or rather the victorious story and news they told, changed all the world around them. So that soon a new age, destined for much progress, dawned. Sadly all but one of the disciples were later executed for their faith! If it had all been a fraud, it's doubtful they would sacrifice their lives for it.

To this day, we can read the exploits, adventures, "acts" and perils of these earliest believers. Through shipwrecks and storms, vipers and prisons, they carried on. The first churches were established. And letters of spiritual insight and impact were written, which survive to this day.

During these early days, much persecution had arisen against the new believers. A legal prosecutor and murderer of believers, Paul, was stopped one day by a bright light and the voice of the teacher. He later became the greatest builder of the churches, and the letters he wrote became much of the New Testament.

He took three major missionary journeys, establishing the first 'churches', or groups of believers, which met in some of their homes. And he claimed, that "by the Spirit of God" he became the "apostle to the Gentiles" for it was clearly revealed, the grave had been overcome on behalf of all persons, peoples, and all nations for many of the new converts and churches consisted of many Gentiles of ancient Greece.

The New Testament was written in the romantic and dramatic language and style of Greece, and the new age that followed, was built upon Roman-Greco roots, the gospel victory message and promise, and upon the acts of these early believers.

The "Book of Acts" is the story of Peter, and James and others of the 'church' centered in Palestine, and of Paul the missionary to the non-Jewish nations, and his three journeys mostly through Asia Minor (today Turkey) and Greece, establishing the earliest groups of "brothers and sisters". Then he went on to Rome and had two spells in the Roman prison, where he continued to write letters (or "Epistles") and continued to teach and build up the church, the believers.

CHAPTER 3 ~ THE FIRST LETTERS

We have, in our possession, letters of the very first Christian believers. They make many awesome and profound declarations, claiming to be written under the "inspiration of the Holy Spirit" the supreme power, and Great Spirit and spark of Life...

All the letters together, span a time of about fifty years. In the New Testament, Paul's letters are listed first, then other letters by other writer's, but surely if we read them in the order they were written, a continuous story may emerge.

JAMES - There's actually three men named James, who were close to Jesus. There's James, a disciple, and the "brother of John" (also a disciple, the "sons of Zebedee"); and James, "the son

of Alphaeus", who was also a disciple;
and there was also James, the "brother of
Jesus" who became very involved in the
church after the crucifixion and
resurrection. He became one of the
leaders of the church in Jerusalem, along
with Peter, and was a member of the
"Jerusalem Council" which made some
important early decisions, and he likely is
the author of this letter written to Jewish
Christians "scattered about", telling them
to welcome the troubles and storms of
life, as well as the calms, for testing
brings endurance, strength and wisdom.
Don't be tossed around by the winds of
earth and change, for God is
unchangingly good, and casts no shifting
of shadows as do other things throughout
the course of the day, beneath the blazing
sun. We are His precious children and He
has given us His Word about life. James
writes we should shun anger, and pray for

the Spirit to control our tongue, for it is a beast! And can set things on fire!

Prejudism or favoritism, and love of the world and status, is a trait of the lower nature, as is bickering and harsh words, and we should rather, "be true", for true faith is what transforms both the heart and life, and brings forth the good fruit(s) of the gospel news. If we hear, but do not do, we are not really believing, for true faith will bring forth changes and results in us and in our life.

1 THESSALONIANS - Some early believers had died, and wouldn't you know it, the question had arisen, especially in Thessalonica, whether the dead believers were safe! Paul wrote and assured them. When Jesus returns, he will resurrect and bring our believing loved ones with him.

2 THESSALONIANS - Paul had written so well, impressing upon the

Thessalonian believers how Jesus could return at any given moment, that many of the Thessalonians had ceased to work and earn their daily bread! And now were going about having fallen into gossip and other idle pursuits! So Paul wrote a second letter, telling them they should work to support their own needs, and should live quiet, non meddlesome lives, worthy of the Lord, for no one but the Father knows when Jesus will be returning to rebuild paradise.

CHAPTER 4 ~ MORE
ANCIENT LETTERS

GALATIANS - Overbearing ones were trying to convince the small group of believers of Galatia, who were Greek, and thus Gentile (and had been practicing pagans all thier lives) that they now had to follow the Judean commandments, of the Old Covenant or Testament (plus added manmade ones) in order to be saved/live on after death.

Paul wrote, asserting, if we depend upon our efforts to 'be good', we will most assuredly fail and "be lost"! It is by faith and grace (by His transforming Holy Spirit POWER in us) that we are saved, transformed and grow in peaceful grace.

Thus we are not to allow ourselves to be shackled by any other teaching, no matter how great or wonderful, for, bottom line, such things are ineffective.

The Law was/is the all important 'babysitter' of the old man. But in Christ, the old man dies (is "crucified with Christ"). And we are now to be a new person, one who is filled with and "led by the Spirit" and is also coming more and more under the control of God's own (Holy) Spirit, the only effective grace.

1 CORINTHIANS - Corinth was a very large metropolitan city, close to Athens. Later, in the seven "letters to the seven churches of Asia" in the first three chapters of the prophetic Book of Revelation, we can see that the predominant moral temptation of those days had to do with, you guessed it, sex. For a 'new' pagan 'Christianity' had emerged, with many branches embracing the old views, ways and practices of the old religions, which included sex rites.

And so it was, in 'sophisticated' Corinth, that a ranking member, of the Corinth group, a leader, was having an affair with another married member. And no one seemed to think anything of it. So Paul wrote addressing this problem, and other issues which had arisen. It's important to live honorable lives! And to fully follow the faith. Selfish living and gratification, only leads to destruction (falling-apart-ness), unhappiness, (all) death and dissatisfaction. (Which actually is the crux of mankind and Earth's curse to begin with! Once thinking ability and thus choice, was endowed, this present journey and lesson was pretty much unavoidable.)

ROMANS - Paul wrote to the believers at Rome, for he was planning to visit. He had not been there before, and did not know the Roman believers, so he introduced himself, and summarized his

insights and teachings of the Good
Tidings of Salvation (rescue!) from the
curse of death. Which curse, shadows this
land and life seeing as "the whole
creation groans". This book "Romans" is
said to be the great 'legal' document on
the tenets of the Christian faith.

2 CORINTHIANS - Now that the
believers had disciplined and (somewhat
gently) rebuked the miscreants of their
group, Paul now wrote for them to
welcome these ones wholeheartedly back
into the faith and friendship, as they had
seen the error of their ways, and changed
their course. And it would not be good
(nor Christian) to alienate them and hold
a grudge, or superiority, or spirit of
judgement against them. Rather we
should comfort others with the same
comfort (from the Spirit) that we
ourselves have been comforted with.
(Surely the spirit of forgiveness and

grace, all of us having been born into
imperfection/selfishness.)

CHAPTER 5 ~ SOME LATER
LETTERS FROM PAUL

PHILEMON - Paul wrote this letter to
a fellow Christian named Philemon. This
letter reveals a beginning of the
breakdown of prejudice and
discrimination. An indentured 'slave' was
now, as a Christian, an equal in class, and
a fellow believer. In the New Way, all are
of one universal family, for elsewhere
Paul wrote, "in Christ, there is neither Jew
nor Greek, male nor female, freeman nor
slave".

We may have differing roles and
places in life, but we are equal in status
in the eyes of God. Jesus sowed the seeds
of peaceful change.

COLOSSIANS - Paul was in Prison in
Rome, when a brother rushed in to see

him and report the news of a "Colossian Heresy". Epaphras, upon visiting the group in Colossae, had found them worshiping angels and 'cosmic powers', rather than the Father and the Son.

Paul, from his jail cell wrote to the Colossians reminding them of the miraculous events which occurred when they had received the good news, and how the good news was moving through the world doing these same supernatural things in many places. Wasn't it Jesus who brought them alive and blessed them in all these ways? And Jesus is ruler over all angelic and cosmic, or heavenly powers. He wanted them to understand that nothing comes close to comparing to Jesus, the only proclaimed "Son of God". We couldn't be more privileged! We couldn't fly any higher.

Paul reminds them of how the Father declares that all things began in the Son,

and all things are being gathered back
into the Son. We "sit in heavenly places
with Christ Jesus". We should not settle
for anything less! But should have
confidence in the power and scope of the
cross, having every right and expectation
to the highest calling.

They were to share their letter with
the group of believers at Laodicea, and
read and share the letter he'd written to
the Laodiceans (which we do not have!
There have been new writings and
gospels found, but they have been found
to have been written as late as 400 A.D.
and are largely believed to have
originated with the pagan 'Christian'
groups, as the themes and spirit of these
writings differ greatly from the traditional,
widely circulated among the early church,
New Testament ones.)

EPHESIANS - The town of Ephesus
was right in the middle of some major

trade routes in West Asia Minor (these days, Turkey). So it was a bustling commercial center. It was also a center for religion and learning. Greek society was very much into philosophy and ideas, religions, discussion, speaking and learning. Ephesus had a renowned city university and library, and a prominent temple to "Diana".

Paul established a school in Ephesus, where the tenets of the still new, Christian faith were taught. He lived and taught there for two years.

One day in the public square a large crowd of Ephesians became a mob and kept shouting "Diana!" "Diana!" "Diana!" And dragged two of the brothers into the courtyard to be declared criminals and beat, or even killed. All this, because a maker of statues had stirred some folks up against the faith, for it was causing him to make less profit for he sold statues of Diana for worshiping.

But after a few hours of yelling, the crowd quieted and it all came to nothing. Acts, chapter nineteen, tells us these things, and that most of the people in the crowd didn't know why they were yelling or why they were there! And some were yelling about one thing, and some another!

This Book of Ephesians is the letter Paul wrote to the christians who lived at Ephesus. Later, when Paul had set his course for mighty Rome, he stopped on the way at the shore near Ephesus. For Paul knew he would never be returning from his trip to Rome. The Ephesian church met them on the beach, and they spent a little time together worshiping and praying, then, embracing with tears, they walked Paul and his companions to their ship, and bid them farewell and Godspeed..

Paul wrote to the Ephesians of how we should drink deeply of the Spirit, and be filled up with him (the Spirit of God, which we access through Jesus). The whole world is destined to be filled with him, he being the fullness which fills all things.

PHILIPPIANS - The letter written to the Philippian believers could be called a book of joy. "Every knee shall bow, and every tongue confess that Jesus is Lord!" and "whether we live or whether we die, we are the Lord's". Paul and this group of believers were close partners, and he thanked them for money sent to help him while he was incarcerated in Rome. Although Paul was in jail, he rejoiced greatly because everyone knew he was in jail just for being a Christian! And because of this, the good news of the Lord, and his resurrection, was becoming widely known!

He also rejoiced in his humble position. Once known for fulfilling all societal and upper crust expectations, he now counts these as nothing, in as much as there is only glory in our Lord – human stature, or goodness (flawed as it is) is completely unreliable and insufficient. Being filled with Jesus is what matters. And what works! He also rejoiced in knowing that the good work God had begun in his dear friends, God would be faithful to carry out to its fulness. If we remain in God, and God in us, we will ever grow in grace, and love will fill and overflow us more and more.

Epaphroditus, a believer from Philippi had been visiting and working with Paul, but had become sick. Paul wrote the concerned Philippians that Epaphroditus was well and eager to return home to them.

CHAPTER 6 ~ LETTERS OF PETER
(AND MORE OF PAUL'S)

1 TIMOTHY - Paul "appointed by God the Father, and Jesus the Lord" wrote this letter to Timothy, a fellow (gospel) worker and traveler, who was at Ephesus, whom Paul had left 'in charge' while he traveled to Macedonia and Greece. He sent a strong reminder, as was his custom to do, warning how false doctrine robs the gospel of its saving power. (We must fight to keep a firm hold on the truth.) A strong heresy was gaining ground at Ephesus. It asserted all matter, and the human body itself is evil, only spirit is good (they must have forgotten how God made the natural world, the fruits and herbs for food, and marriage, and said how it was "all good"). In

Ephesus this error of perception was practiced by an ascetic undue harshness upon the body, but in other places, as with the sect of the "Nicolaitans" it took shape as immorality and vice, for seeing that all physical function was evil, the attitude was that moral actions didn't matter, because everything is evil!

Paul believed it was obvious, our lives need to truly reflect the truth and the peace of the gospel, if the gospel is to remain firm in the world, and in our own inner life.

Paul urged that prayers be said for all people and for those in authority and in earthly offices. He strongly pointed out how Godliness in family and church, is far more advised than wasting time on strange fables, myths, mysteries or old wives tales. We should have our trust in He, who "is the savior of all, especially of those that believe" (verse 4:10).

41

TITUS - Paul had earlier left friend, and fellow worker, Titus, on the Island of Crete to establish and strengthen the churches forming there. Paul knew how man loves to give speeches ("vain talkers" he called them) but Godliness and sound doctrine far exceed the value of "foolish controversies and genealogies, and striving and debates over the law" (and rules) which are not only time consuming, but are completely "unprofitable".

His advice was to avoid debate seeking and divisive believers, for it is better to be fruitful in good deeds.

1 PETER - Peter wrote a letter to believers who were scattered throughout the Roman kingdom. These early believers faced much hardship and persecution. Peter wanted to remind them, that God is in control and is faithful. We live in this world as pilgrims, knowing our home is not man's world but the eternal kingdom. Keeping our eyes upon the Lord, sees us safely through, for remaining close to Him is what leads to holiness. (This is only logical, as surely, God is the only source of holiness, perfection and goodness). Peter urged righteous living, by encouraging the looking forward to, and expectation of the Lord's return to restore paradise/perfection. (Christianity is a philosophy which states death is the anomaly... not life).

2 PETER - Peter wrote a second letter to the believers scattered throughout the Roman lands. He was concerned for their safety, for many false ideas and doctrines were circulating. False teachers had infiltrated the churches, stirring up much trouble. Barring all these false teachings and human ideas and theories, believers in Jesus and the New Testament, can continue in spiritual growth. If we want firm faith and understanding, we should seek to know God more and more. We should not be overly attached to this worldly system, as Jesus is returning soon to overthrow it and establish the Father's Kingdom of goodness and harmony.

2 TIMOTHY - Paul felt that his life would soon be over, and he wanted to address some issues and problems he saw on the horizon. Not only was Paul's sojourn and life coming to a close, but hard and perilous times were coming. Timothy and others were to stand firm, understanding God's sovereign control even in the midst of increasing troubles, persecutions, danger and perils.

Paul himself was back in prison, all his Christian friends had abandoned him and no one had stood up for him. Luke only had remained. Paul wanted Timothy to bring Mark, who was doing good work for him, to Rome, and to bring him some books and parchments he'd left behind, and his cloak. Perhaps he was cold and lonely and had nothing to read! But he affirms that the Lord "stood with him and strengthened him and delivered him from the lion's mouth". As was his custom, he sent greetings to others by name, and he signed off his writing with "the Lord be with your spirit, and grace be with you".

CHAPTER 7 ~ LETTERS OF JUDE, JOHN AND UNKNOWN

JUDE - Who Jude wrote to, is not known. But he urged them to "contend earnestly for the purity of the gospel" and stay safe in God, who would prevent them from falling. He had a very low opinion of those who were trying to change the faith, who believed matter and molecules were the evil and corruption of life. To them, man had fallen into matter, which was what they needed to be rescued from. He called these ones, "spots at your feasts" and "foaming waves of the sea" for they were known for their sexual license. He gave a stern warning of how ancient cities of long ago are an example of eternal punishment, and the smoke of their burning still rises (as everlasting memory).

HEBREWS - The identity of the author of this letter addressed "to the twelve tribes" is uncertain, but like the first chapters of Colossians and Ephesians, the first chapter of this book says some especially awesome things about the Lord, life, and the Father's blueprint for redemption (from imperfection, and its result, death/nonlife).

Jewish believers are advised not to turn back to the letter of the law, for Jesus is the fulfillment of God's promises and purpose. He is forever the spiritual High Priest (counselor, and guide) for us all. What God demands from us, is our trust. Faith is the New Covenant and Way. All the promises are received only through knowing we have them, which is called "faith". It is not a striving to be good, which is effective in transforming the heart and life, but it is God himself, and being filled up with Him. Drawing close to Him, in obedience to the gospel message, is the only transforming and effective grace. Human nature, and pride, may want to hold out hope that there is inherent goodness within that is good enough, but this is actually a "hardening of the heart against God and His gospel" instructions.

1, 2 & 3 JOHN - John, that "beloved" disciple of Jesus, was getting to be an elderly person when he wrote these three short letters. The first urges all believers to "fellowship with the Father". Our salvation is to know Him, and "the One He sent forth", Christ Jesus. The closer our union with the Father and the Son, the more joy, peace, and victory of life we have.

In his second letter, he sums up the

one commandment Jesus left with us,
which is love. We are to love God, and we
are to truly love others.

John's third letter asks us to display
Christian hospitality (welcome) and
friendliness, especially to fellow
Christians.

John addressed fellow believers as
"little children" and often liked to remind
them to "love one another" for "God is
love" (I Jn 4:8).

~ CHAPTER 8 ~
REVELATION / APOCALYPSE

REVELATION(S) - The Book of Revelation, or its Greek name, "Apocalypse", is the story of the consummation of good and evil. Adam and Eve, placed in and of the GARDEN PARADISE had eaten of the forbidden tree of the KNOWLEDGE of both good and evil, which fruit we are still chewing on to this day. (Once thinking ability, thus choice, was endowed, a whole new world, or tree, of possibilities 'came to be'.) In this final book of the Bible, the FRUIT OF THE EARTH is fully ripe, both goodness, and wickedness. John was a very old man, when Roman authorities banished him to an uninhabited island called "Patmos".

While he was there, the Lord Jesus

showed him a great vision of how man's world would end up. The visions of this book are especially poignant. Believers are urged to read, listen to, and hear, the words of this little book – after the mighty crash of all things false and the last great war of nations, Armageddon (with environmental woes as a precursor to these things) and after a 1,000 year Kingdom of our Lord's long second advent of rebuilding paradise upon Earth, the New Jerusalem (the new capital of the planet) comes down from heaven, onto the earth.

It shines of jewels and gold, and the pure sparkling river of the water of life flows through it, to all the world, with trees of life on either side, which leaves and fruit will be for the total healing, and continued health of the nations. No eye will again cry from sorrow, there will be no sickness, suffering or death. The question of good and evil, right and wrong, what is life as opposed to what is death, has been answered for all time, and all citizens have it engraved deeply upon their very hearts and minds for all eternity and ages. To stray from Perfection/Life/God, is to stray away from the very "breath of life" and can only ever end in a self destructive puff of smoke... and dust and ashes.

Elsewhere we are told "eye has not seen, nor ear conceived, nor heart ever been able to fully imagine, all the good things God has created for those who love Him."

CHAPTER 9 ~ ADAM & EVE, NOAH, & MAN'S FIRST TOWER

ADAM & EVE - Adam and Eve were placed side by side in the fruitful garden, the beautiful Garden of Eden. Two races came of their union. But only one race survived the flood.

NOAH - Noah and his family, along with a male and female of every root "kind" of animal, and small flocks of others, safely rode out the waters of the flood in the ark Noah and his sons spent one hundred years building. It was after the waters receded, that God gave the first visible rainbow, as a symbol of beauty, newness and peace, and His promise to not begin over again, no matter how wicked or depraved mankind becomes.

The sons of Noah, and their wives are the ancestors of all families and people living today. The flood caused much sediment and aging under it. All people's have handed down memories of the flood, which have become legends of a great deluge. Much has been made of the fact that some of these were written down before Moses account. But one's memories can be written after another's without plagiarism being involved. Moses' account is missing some outrageous features of other lands, for his account is said to be "inspired by God" rather than handed down merely through the imaginations and embellishments of men.

THE TOWER OF BABEL - Everyone had a common language and worked (somewhat) together. They were building a tower, called Babel Tower, "to reach to the stars," they said. It was built of the red clay of Mesopotamia and Babylonia.

Revelation, refers to the Fall of Babylon, when "all high towers will fall" (Isaiah).

"Look" the Father told the Son, "what man begins to do". If they all work as one, there's no telling what mischief they can accomplish (bringing about destruction). "Let us go down and confuse their languages that they may leave off this building of the tower." As a beneficent parent, and overseer of the "fruit of the earth," the Father has let things (rationality, the ability to make choices) and the world run its natural course, so His children could see, learn and know Truth. It is from Babel Tower that all peoples spread out. What perfect names - Babel and Babylon. For man's works, and the city which grows to fill the earth, echoes with the babel of voices, and absent, is the golden silence and harmony of Paradise.

CHAPTER 10 ~ FOUR
ANCIENT FATHERS

ABRAHAM - After awhile, God called
(to) Abraham who lived at the edge of
Mesopotamia. "Come" he said "it's my
purpose to start a nation, a people apart"
(that men may find the promised "babe"
in the swaddling cloths, which was
Israel). Abraham, it is recorded, was a
righteous man before God, "because he
believed God". And the nation, as we
know, was to be the prepared home for
the Lord Jesus. Through faith (believing)
and the Holy Seed of God, which is Jesus,
Abraham will inherit all nations, for all will
be in Jesus, his grandson of grandsons.

MOSES - As the nation grew, because
of mistakes they made, Israel became
slaves to Egypt; Joseph had been sold

into slavery by his very own brothers! But God blessed him, and thus, in the 'end', he became a "branch which went over the wall, and prospered mightily" (in Egypt). Yet four hundred years later, Moses was used by God, to bring out and deliver them from their great bondage in slavery, a story used to illustrate the whole plan of God, to deliver, rescue, and save us out of death, whose great shadow like Egypt covers the land, and from our capture and enslavement to imperfection, its cause.

DAVID - Later, in the restored nation, David was a young shepherd of sheep (a type of our Lord) who not only ended up writing many of the Psalms, Israel's songs and poetry to "the Mighty One of Israel", but he became a king of Israel, under whom the Hebrew tribes became a great nation. He also had many 'adventures', some of which came about because of bad choices he made; but God (YaHWeH) called him "a man after my own heart", for like all of us, God Himself, declares us righteous, through the "shed blood and sacrifice of Jesus". Ancient religions sought to placate God and remove our distance from the deity, but God Himself provided 'the sacrifice' one dramatic enough to penetrate all psyches and hearts. His grace grounds us, fills us and carries us through, as of course, we are both saved, and transformed, only by grace (the imparting to us, of God's own Spirit, character and likeness, as we ever draw closer and "know Him" more and more, forever).

SOLOMON - God had given to David the plans or blueprint, for the Temple. So far Israel worshiped God collectively in a large beautiful and elaborate tent, or "tabernacle" which had been set up, finally, at Shiloh. But now that they were well settled and established at one place, surely a beautiful Temple to His Glory, was the ideal thing.

But because David had fought too many wars, God decided He would rather David's son, Solomon, carry out the actual building. The Creator was constantly disappointed in the actions of (imperfect) mankind, even in the lives of those He chose to serve Him. But He was kind and forgiving, which is, of course, His very nature and character. Sometimes there were acts and practices which were particularly vile and evil, and God warned (even thunderously) how the judgements, results and consequences were positive to come along.

And sometimes He quickened the judgements for the sake of the innocent, to break up unbelievable patterns of evildoing and suffering. The last straw was when Israel, like nations around it, laid living babies and children in fire. A horrific thing which came about because of the strange sex rite worship practices they had adopted, which brought about many unexpected babies.

About this offering of children to 'gods' through fire, God said "It never came from my mind or heart" this burning of people!

CHAPTER 11 ~ THE RINGING VOICE OF THE PROPHETS

THE PROPHETS - God's words of judgements and prophecies are recorded and grouped together at the end of the Old Testament. There were national prophecies for Israel and for other nations; both immediate to their day, and also as 'latter day' prophecies for the "Day of The Lord", along with visions of a following future paradise kingdom. Always the answer to any judgement, was the prophecies and promises of the redeemer, which were always blended or lumped together, both the prophecies of His first advent (coming) and His second advent and coming, as though it were to all occur at once. In this same way, former and latter prophecy is blended, and parallel, having both (a more or less) 'immediate' fulfillment, and also a 'last days' or end of days fulfillment.

ISAIAH 7:14 - "Therefore the Lord himself shall give you a sign; Behold, a virgin shall conceive, and bear a son..." ["The angel Gabriel told her (Mary).. you shall conceive a son.. called Son of the Most High, and the Lord God will give Him the throne of His father David, and He shall reign over the house of Jacob forever" from Luke 3:26-33.]

1 KINGS 9:5 - "Then I will establish the throne of your kingdom over Israel forever, as I promised David your father, saying, "You shall not fail to have a man on the throne of Israel." Jesus is on that throne and all nations, peoples, tongues and cultures are said to be "grafted into Israel", a new name for God's Kingdom and paradise.

ISAIAH 9:7 - "Of the increase of His

government and peace there will be no end, upon the throne of David and over His kingdom, to order it and establish it with judgment and justice from that time forward, even forever..."

The Prophets, from ancient times, told us the Promised Messiah and Rescuer, would be "born of a maiden" (which were virgins, in that day, that nation) - would be pursued into Egypt, "born in Bethlehem", "a Light in Galilee, by the way of the sea", would come "humble and riding on the colt of a donkey", and would suffer. The New Testament records "he was wounded for our transgressions, and by His whip lashes we are healed", and He would save His people from their sins, to list just a few of the prophecies made by the prophets. ("God is the savior of all, especially those which believe" 1 Timothy 4:10.)

MALACHI 4:5,6 - "Behold, I will send

you the spirit of Elijah"
(prophecy/truth/coming collapse) "before
the Great Day of the LORD. He will turn
the hearts of the fathers to the children,
and the hearts of the children to the
fathers, lest the earth be utterly
destroyed." [These dramatic words, are
the last words of the Old Testament.]

JOEL 2:29 - "I will pour out my Spirit
upon all flesh. Your sons and your
daughters shall prophecy, your old men
will dream dreams, your young men will
see visions, also on my menservants and
my maidservants shall I pour out my
Spirit in those days."

MALACHI 4:1,2 - "The day comes
which shall burn as an oven and all
evildoing will be as stubble, leaving
neither root nor branch" (to ever rise
again) "but unto you who reverence my
name shall the Sun of Righteousness
arise with healing in His wings, and you

shall leap" (for joy) "like calves released from the stall."

MICAH 4:3,4 - "The Lord will judge between many peoples, and will rebuke strong nations. They shall beat their weapons into plows, and their spears into pruning shears. Nation shall not lift up sword against nation. Neither shall they learn war anymore. But they shall abide each one under their own vine" (and fruit trees!) "and no one will bother them."

JEREMIAH 31:12,13,14 - "Therefore they shall come and sing in the height of Zion, and shall flow together to the goodness of the LORD... their soul shall be as a watered garden; and they shall not sorrow anymore at all. Then shall the maiden rejoice in the dance, along with both young men and old, for I will turn their mourning into joy, and will comfort them, and make them rejoice from their sorrow. I will satiate the soul of the priest" (believer) "with fatness, and my people shall be satisfied with my goodness, saith the LORD."

JEREMIAH 31:3 - "Yea, I have loved thee with an everlasting love, therefore with loving kindness have I drawn thee."

JEREMIAH 33:3 - "Call unto me, and I will answer you and show you great and mighty things, which thou knowest not.."

And.. **REVELATION 21:5** - "Behold, I will make all things new."

ISAIAH 11:6-9 - "The wolf will dwell with the lamb. The bear will be seen grazing with the cow, and the lion will eat straw like the ox. There shall be no hurting, because knowledge of the Lord will cover the earth like the waters cover the seas."

POSTSCRIPT....

According to bible prophecy, the dismantling or destruction of the Wailing Wall begins a countdown. [For bible scholars – Daniel 12:11,12.]

A countdown of forty-two, thirty day months, after which will occur forty-five days of great shortage, with the last ten days (Rev. 2:10) being mortally critical (or that is to say, what the bible calls a time of great tribulation).

A PREVIEW of "A NEFARIOUS PENTAGRAM"

CHAPTER ONE
THE 'END' IS NOT YET

When the first angelic mind began to ponder a different universe than God's, apocalypse began. And ever since Cain slew Abel, a nefarious, and ghostly edifice and potential has been slowly, but surely, taking shape in our world. Through the ages of civilization, this diabolical structure has been growing, block upon block, pentagram upon pentagram, with its final face being the crowning achievement, (the true conspiracy) and the shadowy results of millennia.

The "Book of Revelation" or "Apocalypse" reveals this ghostly structure in a colorful and majestic vision which was seen and recorded by John the Apostle in his old age when he was banished to the uninhabited Island of Patmos. Dramatic events are portrayed in sequence and series like a symphony of visions upon a lavishly set stage.

Like thick velvet curtains slowly parting, "Apocalypse" reveals its secrets, and if we will settle back as if in ringside theater seats, we will soon hear a thunderous noise of approaching hoof beats. Four powerful and notorious horses, with riders, gallop steadily across the stage, stirring up clouds of dust and sand as they go. They are howling winds upon the stage of time. Our hair blows back from our faces, and sand stings our eyes and coats our teeth. They soon dwindle from our sight. But what we want to remember is these "Four Horsemen of the Apocalypse" once they begin their ride, continue their gallop throughout the whole (Revelation) production, with each gallop becoming more thunderous and pronounced at the 'end'. It is in their winds, that the rest of the Apocalypse visions occur.

Where may the world we live in be heading? Where might it be in fifty years or less from now? Peering through the mists of the future, what potentially awaits mankind?

Better than Nostradamus, more accurate than Edgar Cayce, the mysterious and infamous "Book of Revelation" is a window to the world of tomorrow, perhaps a world just around the corner, certainly a world whose foundations can be glimpsed today. It was written almost two thousand years ago, yet within its pages can be found the answers for today! For if we are able to read its warnings, perhaps we can apply the brakes, lest mankind rush quickly into the perils and cataclysms it so vividly portrays. To do this, we must understand its mysteriously cloaked message.

One of the intricate keys to reading

this mystic message, is to realize, and fully understand, that all its visions play out to the utter end of the last act, each vision being like the musical note of a song, which once begun, continues to sound til the very end of the apocalyptic composition. The story is classic good versus evil, indeed it is the peak of good and evil, and a frozen moment and snapshot of it.

In this epic production, it's the bad guys who steal center stage. They didn't begin as villains. People built them, and contributed to them, with the best of intentions. But over time, they expand, and develop a life and essence all their own, until one day they are seen to all rear up with a mighty roar.

"Apocalypse" is the drama that flows out from them. Seeing them early, is our warning, and even though they are phantoms, they're easy to see if we realize they are the biggest influences which are working upon humanity and the world today. They begin, grow and endure. Everything runs its course, then suddenly, at the end of the vision, with a flourish, they're gone, and are replaced by a green and lush world of fruit filled trees and sparkling rivers, where "the lion will eat straw like the ox, and the bear will graze with the cow". [Isaiah 11:7]

The Revelation narrative, is a complete drama of the ages. It's the story of human history as a whole, the story of all peoples, and every nation, and it's the story of every individual. Like holding mirror up to mirror, producing the mirage of a long hallway – the many stories of life, are the one story, repeated over and over. And it's the lesson and drama being written upon every heart. But the revelation climax is not a set schedule. It can happen sooner, or later. It's a constant war, a war of good and evil.

CHAPTER TWO
NOTORIOUS HORSEMEN

In the prophetic theater of "Apocalypse" we see a scene in the starry heavens – a glorious and mighty throne is surrounded by flashes of lightning, smoke and huge, heavenly creatures singing "holy, holy, holy" along with myriads of winged angels as far as the eye can see. We watch, as the Lamb of God, the Lord, the only Begotten, is given a rolled up scroll. This is a long scroll, rolled and bound with a series of "seven seals" with the first seal being visible, for it closes, like a sticker, the end of the scroll. Each seal will be broken, allowing portions of the scroll to be unrolled and progressively read. It is when the Lamb breaks open the first seal, that the Revelation story truly begins. [Rev 5:1-7; 6:1]

The four horsemen we saw galloping, are the first four seals on this scroll. They are galloping, because their influence is on the gallop. That is to say, they increase. Each one, along with the rest of the seven seals, are seven advancing elements, which gallop and pick up momentum through the latter age, the latter age being the years of our Lord, A.D.

When with dramatic, and heavenly fanfare, the Lamb breaks the first seal, an angel cries "Come!" and the first horseman of the apocalypse comes riding out upon the wide expanse of the earth. He is upon a white horse, and he is given a crown and a bow, and he goes out conquering and to conquer. [This one is said to have a twin, a shadow, a fifth horseman if you will.] This conqueror began his gallop, at the dawning of the age (of our Lord A.D.) as the spreading gospel of our Lord and Savior. It changed a large slice of the world, even becoming a world! Conquering the old 'gods' and "triumphing openly over them". [Colossians 2:15] This horse and rider is unique, in that almost from the beginning of his ride, he *has* had a parallel rider, who gallops alongside him throughout the age, and then accelerates toward the 'end' right along with him, even overshadowing him! The parallel rider of course is a counterfeit gospel, one which is reborn into the world "coming in unawares", or what we today would call, "on the sly". [Jude 4]

This scroll of seven seals is the revelation narrative. And remember! Each seal, and every vision within them, and vision within vision, play out til the 'end' like an increasing crescendo of them all. This is in the same manner in which each of the four horsemen of the apocalypse, once they begin to ride, continue their gallop right to the end of the age. [Rev 6:1,2]

Meanwhile, back in the starry expanse of the heavens, the second seal on the scroll is broken, and more of the scroll is unrolled. An angel cries "Come!" and a second rider comes forth, sitting upon a galloping red horse, its hoofs, stirring up the dust of time. This horse and rider "has power to take peace from the earth". And he has, during this age, and all ages, for this one is "war". And "war" has been mankind's constant unwanted companion. The red horse's rider is "given a great sword" for his weaponry has been a growing pageant (also). Some bible translations say of this red horse and rider called war – "he is given a long sword". [Rev 6:3,4]

www.ingramcontent.com/pod-product-compliance
Lightning Source LLC
LaVergne TN
LVHW091207080426
835509LV00006B/878

9 780615 235875